Many Appetites

Jason Gordon

*For Jack,
As the great James Tate once said,
"If you're gonna be weird, be all the way weird."*

SPUYTEN DUYVIL
New York City

Acknowledgments

Acknowledgement is made to the journals in which the following poems appeared:

Blue and Yellow Dog ("I hate rain; I sink through," "My eye isn't naked," "The future is broken," "The lady in the moon," "); *Cleaver* ("Even dogs have feelings even fleas," "I try not to explode," "It's still December still July," "You steal my hubcaps"); *CutBank* ("I can throw a pumpkin full of explosives," "I have no lungs," "It takes years to write one report days to write one word seconds to write one life story," "My coffee tastes like piss"); *Presa* ("A field with grass so dead," "No one can see the future," "The mind is a dark ocean of voices," "The only cloud," "The stars carve circles in the sky," "You wake up at midnight; the moths"); and *Yes, Poetry* ("Born, unborn," "I can't sleep; I'm becoming," "I love the beach even though it's a giant litterbox/ashtray," "Is this how the world ends, angels inside us," "It's stupid to believe in miracles," "The angel in the phone line," "The window is open, just enough," "Sleep provides energy for the day's undertakings").

Portions of "cave drawings" appeared in *Pretty Owl* and *Skidrow Penthouse*.

Portions of "lost in st. texas" appeared in *Switchback* and *The American Journal of Poetry*.

I would also like to thank Pudding House Publications for printing a selection of these poems, *I Stole a Briefcase,* as part of their chapbook series.

Additionally, I am grateful to the editors of Ravenna Press for publishing many of these poems in the chapbook, *Attack of the Nihilist*, as part of their Triplets Series.

© 2019 Jason Gordon

ISBN 978-1-949966-54-1

Library of Congress Cataloging-in-Publication Data

Names: Gordon, Jason, 1979- author.
Title: Many appetites / Jason Gordon.
Description: New York : Spuyten Duyvil, 2019. |
Identifiers: LCCN 2019027900 | ISBN 9781949966541 (trade paperback)
Subjects: LCSH: Home--Poetry. | Work--Poetry.
Classification: LCC PS3607.O59373 A6 2019 | DDC 811/.6--dc23
LC record available at https://lccn.loc.gov/2019027900

for Travis

CONTENTS

Attack of the Nihilist

No one can see the future	3
The only cloud	4
You wake up at midnight; the moths	5
The stars carve circles in the sky	6
A field with grass so dead	7
The mind is a dark ocean of voices	8

Holding Myself for Ransom

I have no lungs	11
I can throw a pumpkin full of explosives	12
It takes years to write one report days to write one word seconds to write one life story	13
My coffee tastes like piss	14

String Theories

It's still December still July	17
Even dogs have feelings even fleas	18
You steal my hubcaps	19
I try not to explode	20

Oneirology

The window is open, just enough	23
Sleep provides energy for the day's undertakings	24
It's stupid to believe in miracles	25
I love the beach even though it's a giant litter box/ashtray	26
Is this how the world ends, angels inside us	27
The angel in the phone line	28
Born, unborn	29
I can't sleep; I'm becoming	30

cave drawings   31

Fragile Little World

My wife came home and   41
The paperboy fired one at me while riding   42
Navy SEALs   43
Little hole-in-the-wall tavern   44
Us men in suits   45
A huge fireball crashed into the house   46

Neuropoem   49

Cheat Codes

The pillow swallows the head   53
I won't look in the mirror my reflection   54
Can you turn off your breasts they're cold   55
The sky is dead   56

Weathervanes

The lady in the moon   59
The future is broken   60
My eye isn't naked   61
I hate rain; I sink through   62

lost in st. texas   63

Attack of the Nihilist

No one can see the future,

not even people
with owls on their heads; but

I can make lightning
strike the barn.

I can fill a boot
with sawdust and
grab a fistful of
white beetles
from my pocket.

What can you do?

The only cloud—

a big cat. It yawns until
its jaws bend backwards and
it swallows its own head.
We often exchange
yawns on the phone.
The star of sex
fades in your eyes;
the dream lays its black
eggs in your hair.
Dust settles on the furniture
of my life. I look out the window:
a swarm of bees
in the shape of a man
walks a puppy down the sidewalk.

You wake up at midnight; the moths

fluttering around the moon,
the moths of your dream, already
begin to fade. There is nothing you can do.
You close your eyes; there is only
darkness, so cold not even
candles of bone could survive.

You stare at the ceiling
which stares back like
the blank page of a book.

The stars carve circles in the sky

like grooves in a record.
Music makes the clouds sad;
they sink into the earth
like the ghosts of our furniture.

But one of them sneaks into
my room while I sleep,
fogging up the mirror with
its breath, placing stones soaked
in moon blood all around my bed.

In the morning I find blue footprints on the ceiling.

A FIELD WITH GRASS SO DEAD

a downpour of angel tears
couldn't revive it. That's where
dreams go when we forget them—

tornados searching for
empty wine bottles to sleep in.

The clouds eat the stars.

The Mind Is a Dark Ocean of Voices

I hear screams; the pinecones
explode like grenades.
The flying squirrels slowly
glide to earth, then
they explode too.

The chandelier swings wildly in my heart.
I stick a fork in my thigh
and somewhere in India
my pain appears on a map.

So many emaciated cows;
the milkman rings the doorbell but
there is no door, not even
a window to climb through.

The moon drops grand pianos from its eyes.

Holding Myself for Ransom

I have no lungs

I breathe by
opening and
closing my fists

I can throw a pumpkin full of explosives

into the kitchen

I can crush a cube of frozen paint thinner in my hand,
lay down on a domino the size of a mattress.

I can rip apart the garden shears
like a wishbone—

angels bouncing between spark plugs,
smoke doing its rain dance around the room:

no one will notice.
The sun is a junkie's eyeball and

rats stampede through the neighborhood.
I play chess against myself.

Every black pawn I take
I have to swallow.

It takes years to write one report days to write one word seconds to write one life story

I make up all my memories—
a blizzard of stars swallowing every weatherman
not armed with an umbrella. Which beers

taste less bad? How do I pry
the inner-squirrel from my finger and
who sent this arresting bouquet
of snorkels? Death?

The grandfather clock
sinks deep into the floor,
its white roots gripping the pipes
like an octopus. I break

and un-break the dishes.

My coffee tastes like piss

and my piss tastes like coffee.
It's the same every morning:
the house folds itself up like a map when I leave it,
static infecting the radio.

I wake the avocado not a real avocado
one from the garden where our ghosts hide.

I'm bored with my eyes,
I close them open them pull off my lips kiss my own nose,
the salad tongs in my hand.

String Theories

It's still December still July

a blue cloud walks a dog across the lake

my hands fall off
I glue them back on
my head falls off
I warm it in the oven

I no longer exist I will
exist again tomorrow

I can't remember
my name can you
remember my name?

it's cold in the microwave

Even dogs have feelings even fleas

but fleas are not important
the Stanley Cup is important
energy drinks are important
lighter fluid is important it makes
fire for smoking pot and pot is
important God is important
he has feelings he has blue
fleas in his beard this isn't
the 60s or it is he can't tell
time his bones dance on the sea

You Steal My Hubcaps

I buy them back
you eat a peach
with a fork made of blood

it's an old heart it weeps
each tear is a seed
or a metaphor for something maybe
love or the sadness of trees

leaves shaped like hands
hands shaped like leaves

your hubcaps my hubcaps

inner-child outer-child
mirror image
                reflection

it's a roadmap crumpling
un-crumpling in the dark

I TRY NOT TO EXPLODE

or microwave the dog

but sometimes the universe
is fucked-up static

a blizzard of stars

antimatter moonlight

so dead it's alive
and infested with clouds

angry clouds full of lightning and snow

cold dandruff
yellow cocaine

angels vacuuming
the lawn I try not
to snort them I try

Oneirology

The window is open, just enough

to let the wind come in,
toss some old receipts on the floor,
chase the cat from the bedroom,
turn on the TV. The rest of the house

is asleep, a dream passing from room
to room like a swarm of ghost bees.
It's a sad dream, one that's survived
hundreds of years, feeding on dead mice
and the occasional lost tennis shoe.

Every wall is a different shade of static.

Sleep Provides Energy for the Day's Undertakings

such as shopping for a new spice rack
or chiseling cat mucus off the kitchen floor with a butter knife,
but come nightfall that energy funnels down the cosmic drain
into a dimension where we are all statues
and our voices are red birds that fly from our mouths.
I sit alone in my cave trying to write poetry but
all that comes from my brain is
nonsense: a white bib forgetting
its own tragic lullaby, some shiny butter snails,
a villa sketched by madmen
pounded into a small cube, then one night
a bright slit appears in the sky
and out spew the stars
followed by pink clouds of dust
inside which angels are born like
corn popping in the microwave.

It's Stupid to Believe in Miracles

If threatened, an angel will fall from the sky,
not a sky you want on a picnic
this sky will bite off your leg!
So can there be joy?
The cervix melts like butter,
the baby oozes out.

I LOVE THE BEACH EVEN THOUGH IT'S A GIANT LITTER BOX/ASHTRAY

Ocean noise sounds like radio static, the womb
minus the bass drum of mother's heartbeat.
Sometimes the sand burns my feet but
have you been to the beach when it's cold,
wind blowing out the birthday cakes
in your eyes? It's not Dorothy's Kansas
or the bingo hall of the underworld it's
a postcard written by statues, something wrong
with the clouds so the weatherman unscrambles eggs on his desk.

Is this how the world ends, angels inside us

multiplying like viruses, microwaving our bones?

We burn our inner-children, feed our laundry to the moon,
die asleep on memory foam. No one remembers.

You press the up button, the elevator never arrives.
Is the lobby all that exists

or is there a malfunction in the heavens,
a hand-shaped weed poking up through the sidewalk?

Pain rises from deep inside the earth.
Mirrors shatter, reading glasses on the floor

like stepped-on grasshoppers. So what's
an old book to do? Swallow a hurricane?

If one writes a book on this side of the mirror
on the other side there must exist the opposite of that book—

a book you can read in the dark, a book
made of snow. The roller coasters untangle themselves.

The Angel in the Phone Line

swims backwards. I've un-dreamt my life: half dead, half drunk.
One morning I'm a cloud in my father's belly; the next a ghost, a
spray of cologne. The scent of the moon making love to the sea.
The scent of two storms making love on the beach. I can't decide.
The angel swims forwards, backwards at the speed of darkness.
The more I drink, the louder the dial tone.

BORN, UNBORN

Born again

Dead, undead

I splash coffee on my face, drink a bottle of mouthwash for breakfast

I ejaculate my sorrows into the sink

Into the sea

Sperm the size of whales, whales the size of sperm

I can't sleep; I'm becoming

an owl, an owl with moon-eyes,
an owl who eats pizza for breakfast,
cold pizza with mushrooms of blood.

I disassemble the cuckoo clock
in its nest of brass twigs.

Ghosts piss my name in the snow.

cave drawings

ghosts can't see me

I'm not wearing pants

the moose made of stars

feeds on flies

in the phone booth

my shadow of flies

their wings shoot sparks

---

the heart needs a raincoat the heart needs a cake
to jump out of a stripper the heart never
burps on mars or laughs the heart has pride
in its weird little bubble no crater
named dan the news on mute cops
throwing their guns through a hole in the sky

---

you have a paperclip shaped like
a car in your pocket the piano
on the cat I forgot how to play
makes a song when I'm stoned
and full of blue hummus
the cops don't mind their guns

stab my brain please do not
drive away it reminds them
to breathe

---

a drinking town with a fishing problem

the clouds drop anchors
of glass through the trees

---

the clouds drop children made of snow
down the chimney a ghost clogs the toilet
I'm scared you will leave I grow
sheep in my beard it takes only
a second the children melt slow

---

so many dimensions in the universe

only one dream passing from room
to room peeling paint of walls
exposing cave drawings from the future

or infinite dreams
filling one room
with blue smoke

I close my eyes I no longer exist
I exist in the dimension of god dog particles

god is dead
dog is in heaven

---

oh hidden cameras of fate

the cluster-fuck of scars
in the parking lot
                    is me

I fall never must in love

---

the lady in the moon grows a long
beard of chains there are non-existent
clouds a light bulb crushed into
snow on the lawn I am trying not
to breathe or use the phone to
burn the mind it cannot have
ideas birds flapping in my soup

---

clouds shaped like brains

brains shaped like cows
eating grass on the ceiling

---

like ghosts in a vacuum cleaner
the clouds are all dizzy

the phone in my brain
made of whiskey turns green

the phone is dead

                                          the phone isn't dead

                                          the deer eating comic books
                                          never wears ties

the gods are wireless

---

the deer wake up shake the laundry
from their antlers the moon
burns the lawn we grow old
so quietly little pac-man in
his lamp please do not make
a wish he will eat all my bones

---

the sofa folds into a deathbed

unable to sing or translate
the wind the auto-tuned
birds have all flown away

I dust-bust my beard
pour salt on the plants

                                        I'm not wearing pants
                                        this is not fucking prom

I'm gurgling moonlight

                                        let me start over

anti-thought
ant idea

---

eating flakes from a box

                    on a sofa with ants
             rolling sugar off my skin

      cures everything
              post-postmodern

     like sadness

---

man eats animal
man eats spirit animal

---

why can't all of us sleep on this
little blue pizza the ghost
in the empty skull of pickles
smokes beer I have glue
in my hair a tree tells a joke
in the woods no one hears
I don't laugh or exist
skipping stones shaped like
smiles

Fragile Little World

My wife came home and

shook me from my nap
on the couch. "Is this all you've done
with yourself today?" she asked.
Her hair was disheveled
and full of sawdust, and her apron
was stained with grease
and what looked like blood.
I stared at her, speechless.
She stormed off.
I lay there for awhile longer, then
slowly sat up and brushed
the cookie crumbs from my chest.
I found her in the kitchen
furiously chopping celery.
"Rough day?" I asked.
She didn't respond.
I walked up behind her and
looked over her shoulder.
"What's for dinner?" I asked.

The paperboy fired one at me while riding

his bike past my house. I didn't have time
to duck or to throw my arms up in defense before
it stung me right in the face. I was dazed for a
moment. I reached down for the paper and,
with a primal grunt, hurled it back in his direction.
It toppled end-over-end through the air,
struck him square in the back, making him wobble
out of control and wipe out onto the pavement.
I ran over and pulled the bike off him. He was
wincing in pain and I saw he had a nasty scrape
on his knee, so I took him in my arms and rushed
back into the house. I sat him down in the kitchen,
cleaned the gravel out of his wound and wiped it
with peroxide. I couldn't even look him in the eyes
but I knew he was crying from all his sniffling
and the quiver in his breathing. "I'm sorry,"
he murmured. "No I'm sorry," I confessed.
"It's no wonder you did what you did with examples
like me in the world." I applied a band-aide with
a cartoon squirrel on it and he cracked a little smile.
I smiled too. I walked him back outside,
helped him onto his bike, and watched proudly
for awhile as he pedaled down the street.

Navy SEALs

At 0900 we reported to the beach where
the Master Chief issued each of us a surfboard.
He then sat down under an umbrella
and began to read some sappy romance novel.
We just stood there staring at him, then
at each other. It occurred to me
this was a test, so I stripped down
to my briefs and ran into the ocean.
The other men followed my lead as
I paddled for my first wave. I felt it roll
beneath me, so I slowly got to my feet; but
after only a few seconds I lost my balance
and was crushed by a huge wall of water,
badly scraping my leg on the bottom.
Like a good soldier, I tried again, and again
I wiped out. This went on for hours.
Finally I tucked my board under my arm
and staggered back onto dry sand.
I turned to see the other men pulling off
all kinds of aerial stunts. "I just don't have
what it takes, sir," I said. The Master Chief
sipped a tall glass of pink lemonade.
"That's alright," he replied. "At least
keep the surfboard." "I really don't want
the surfboard," I said. The Master Chief
shot out of his chair. "I order you
to keep the surfboard!" He lifted his sunglasses
and winked. I took the surfboard home.

Little hole-in-the-wall tavern

On lonely nights I'd go in and order a few shots
of whiskey. There was never a lot of business,
just a few gruff-looking regulars that sat at the bar
and stared at whatever game was on TV. So
the bartender must have seen me as a fresh ear
to complain to. He'd start about how his wife
had left him, how he'd been audited by the IRS,
how his bookie wanted to kill him, how his dog
was run over by a truck, how his bad back made it
impossible to even tie his shoes, how his house
was contaminated with a rare toxic mold, etc.
However, the last time I was there some new guy
was working behind the bar. When I asked him
where the usual bartender was he smirked
and told me how he'd won millions playing the lottery.
How he'd moved to some huge villa down in
Miami Beach and no one had heard from him since.
I left without even ordering a drink, and later
lay in the dark, never feeling more alone.

Us men in suits

The lit elevator button
turned into a glowing moth.
We ducked and shielded
our faces until it landed
on a little girl's finger.
"There's nothing to be afraid of,"
she said, before it
coughed out a tiny
puff of black smoke.

Oh how we screamed.

A HUGE FIREBALL CRASHED INTO THE HOUSE

across the street. A crowd flocked to
the scene as a convoy of sirens and
flashing lights arrived. A news crew
approached me, and a well-groomed
young woman with a microphone
asked me what happened. I told her
a flying saucer went down—that
it was spying on our town for years.
She smirked at the cameraman.
"Do you think the aliens survived?"
she asked me. I ran back home and
slammed the door. Later
the news never mentioned the fire.
I suspected the aliens were taken to
some secret laboratory in the desert—
that if alive, they'd be tortured.
I wept, remembering their visits—
how we'd sip tea 'til dawn.

Neuropoem

1.
The living zombie in the machine I call home wears my pants.
Not me I've been never that stoned. I have even ideas.
I die I go to China where I learn to make chickens.
I get seasick reading poems about boats, wake up
naked next to a woman I assume is my wife. She's
not the Great Wall. She vomits pink foam, I eat my own brain.

2.
I unfold my brain and crumple it into a ball.
My brain is a paper swan that wants to be a real swan.
A ganglia of morons. It eats this poem
it vomits this poem. This poem isn't edible.
It can't lie or tell the truth. Ask me about this poem,
this peom. Pretend your brain loves mine
or my brain hates cures. Yours thinks
better than mine, types fast with slow errors.
It's not also worse at perpendicular parking.

Cheat Codes

THE PILLOW SWALLOWS THE HEAD

but the mind with its tentacles
of blue light rests on a nest
of crumpling un-crumpling poems

or it sits on the TV and stares at
the tree growing out of the sofa

it doesn't wear pants it can't
think or hum songs from the 80s

too much not enough
synthesized drums

too asleep too awake

it can't decide

I won't look in the mirror my reflection

is a vampire with acne and prescription sunglasses
he stays up all day writing poems about nothing he's not
my mirror image he will never taste lobster
dipped in blood or bend his fork into a bracelet
for you to re-gift like his heart covered in flies

Can you turn off your breasts they're cold

they burn my tongue I can't talk on the phone
or leave silent messages like empty
bottles in the sea like love or hate poems
in my heart your nipples on fire red sky
at night blue moon at noon

The sky is dead

no seeds in the glass
cubes of its teeth

an endless landscape of hiccups
the occasional iceberg
of sunlight taps on the window

oh blank dance of clouds
the porch is on fire
the milk strings of your guitar

shatter on the roof

Weathervanes

The lady in the moon

looks pissed. The clouds
of her breath chase
cars into the lake.

The salmon swim backwards.

The future is broken

Fighter jets disguised as geese assume their checkmark formation
The clouds sink like battleships into the grass
O say can you pee, laughs my inner-child, peeing
Not so funny to the outer-child, prostate swollen, back hair gathering frost
A rose of butter hardens
The beehives die, the snails ask questions

My eye isn't naked,

it wears tiny shoes.

It dances all night
in a puddle of merlot.

Not drunk, not a stone
with quartz teeth

biting the dentist.
This isn't a love poem.

The TV is off, the screen
is a mirror. The dead

leap from clouds shaped like airliners—
falling bodies of rain.

I HATE RAIN; I SINK THROUGH

hours of darkness, passing only
the occasional neon jellyfish.
My bed lands on the moon,
the moon lands on my bed.
It doesn't matter. A cloud
coughs down the door.
I weep, pull a dark quilt
of porn over my eyes.
The dog eats me. Showers
melt the town I grew up in:
the idiot weatherman, his umbrella
opening, closing itself at will.

lost in st. texas

life's a swarm of helicopter seeds

      nowhere is beer not
          hoppy or deranged

            the broken meow
                of a duck in the morning

          can't fit in the brain
      or turn it to stone

the brain wakes up

      skips phones on the lake

            blames mother for wi-fi
        too slow to form thoughts

                the brain's always tired

---

let's exchange brains

      or attempt to give birth
          to each other's bright shadows

      mine is a ghost

a dead spot on the lawn
      in the shape of a man

I build a napkin
  out of swans
  but can't make it swim

    or fall up like a fridge
  full of ghosts
      through the weather

    blue eggs in the brain
      high on stones
        not for breakfast
        the moon
      the brain orbits
       so quietly
         explodes

    I hate yellow ketchup

    I want to believe
  that life isn't boring
      the dust off the furniture

    the windows
in their frames
    expand
      contract
every breath
    so important
        to calm down the flies

      ---

my sponge is a brain
  to squeeze and/or throw

at the cat
> making sounds

>> like a cloud
> giving birth

>> to a phonebook of rain

on the streets of st. texas

> where cops huff paint
>> in the trees
> made of steam

>>> that rise from the manholes

>> that bloom
> in the dark

> where I live in a van
>> or a van lives in me

---

the brain doesn't die
> or dream about math

>> it believes in the absolute
>> value of god

a synapse sparks

> a cloud is born
>> to steal
>> or grow cars

                    on the lake
            of its shadow

    rain rises
    snow globes fall

                the fireflies fail
                        to turn themselves off

                            ---

a spork in the road

            a fork of light

                    in the brain
                            making thunder

            I can't even hear

    the phonebook is dead

                the motherboard on fire

        the wolf in the hamper
                does not watch tv

                                the satellite dish
                    an ear in the sky

            watches me breathe
    inside this weird egg

            I used to call home

                    I cannot remember

                        the doorbell won't sing
                                or require dark powers

I refuse to dance
        like a demonic refrigerator

                with shoes on my hands
                        that dent the wood floor

                my brain
        a collage
                of ideas
                        from the 90s

        that won't come to life
                or sink like old clothes

                                no depth charge can reach
                        blue clouds
                                in the sea

                                still chirps in its nest
                                        of dreams

                stored in temp files

                                ---

blue clouds in the sea
        do not contain thoughts

                        the brain is a frozen
                microwave beeping

                but pizza so cold
                      and folded like laundry

        does not mean I'm dead

    like fish
        in a tree

  unable to translate
      the rustling of leaves

              the rusting of bones

        into silence
     or nonsense

              ---

oh pearl ear of necklaces

            listen to my brain

                    I will not put my phone
                    in a beard of fake birds

so why will I push
    this snowflake
    upstairs
        while not wearing feet
            like a digital human
            like pac-man
      drunk
  on poodles of rain
            in this unplugged machine
                    I call home

                              in the dark

            I know I don't know

      I must first be a sperm

                              underground tornados
                        playing hockey
                                    with the mind

      I must first be an egg

                  the tv is off

                  the tv is watching me
                        sleep on the couch

JASON GORDON earned an MFA from the University of Maryland as well as a scholarship from the Bread Loaf Writers' Conference. He has authored two chapbooks, *I Stole a Briefcase* (Pudding House Publications) and *Attack of the Nihilist* (Ravenna Press). He lives in Catonsville, Maryland, teaching English and creative writing at a middle school for children with dyslexia.

CPSIA information can be obtained
at www.ICGtesting.com
Printed in the USA
BVHW031452260120
570505BV00001B/62